BABY ANIMALS

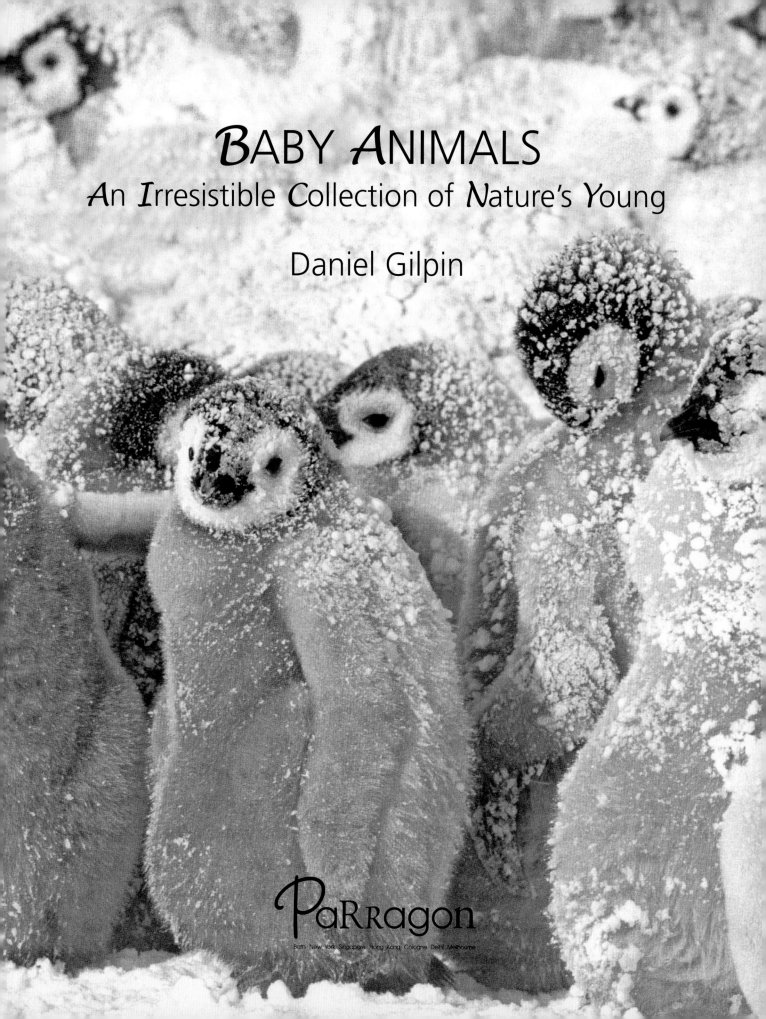

BABY ANIMALS
An Irresistible Collection of Nature's Young

Daniel Gilpin

PaRragon

Bath New York Singapore Hong Kong Cologne Delhi Melbourne

First published in 2008
Parragon
Queen Street House
4 Queen Street
Bath BA1 1HE, UK

Copyright © Parragon Books Ltd 2008

Designed, produced, and packaged by Stonecastle Graphics Limited

Text by Daniel Gilpin
Designed by Sue Pressley and Paul Turner
Picture research by Karen James
Edited by Anthony John

ISBN 978-1-4075-1770-4

Printed in U.A.E.

Contents

Baby Animals

Baby animals are impossible to resist. We are pre-programed to find them adorable. When we look at them, we see the things we see when we look at our own babies: big eyes, round faces, small mouths. Even the way they move makes us smile. We just cannot help ourselves.

The warm feeling we get when we see baby animals is an instinctive reaction to their appearance. It is, in fact, a misplaced emotion, caused by the resemblance of those creatures to babies of our own kind. The more baby animals look like baby humans, the more we feel for them. This is why we find most baby mammals so cute, but feel little for tadpoles, say, or insect larvae. It is because we are mammals ourselves and can see characteristics in those babies and their behavior that we recognize as similar to our own young.

The helplessness of baby animals can make us want to look after them. At the very least we hope that life will treat them well. In short, we briefly feel like parents. This feeling is not confined to adults. Children can experience it too, as anyone who has ever watched a child playing with their pet will know. The human instinct to care for our babies and children is very strong. It is sometimes called the maternal instinct but, as this author can attest, it is not confined to women (although they perhaps feel it more powerfully than men). Nor is this instinct confined only to our own species. Many animal parents, go to great lengths to protect and care for their young.

Baby animals are very vulnerable to predators and most mothers take care to give birth or lay their eggs in as safe a place as possible. Mammals usually try to find a secluded spot in which to give birth. Some dig burrows or find natural holes and caverns that they use as birthing dens. Birds build nests in which to lay their eggs, choosing well-hidden or inaccessible spots. Nests are perched out on the ends of branches or built on the ledges of cliffs. Some birds, like mammals, excavate burrows in which to lay eggs and raise their young. These range from the riverbank tunnels of kingfishers to the holes in trees hammered out by woodpeckers. Others take advantage of natural holes in old trees that they find high off the ground. These may have large entrances and a few species wall these up with mud to make it impossible for predators to get in. Hornbill pairs do this, with the male sealing the female and her eggs inside. She then relies on him to bring her and the hatchlings food, which is passed through a tiny hole in the walled-up entrance. Only once all the youngsters have fledged and are ready to leave the nest is the wall broken down again.

Parental care in many animals extends beyond the first few vulnerable days and weeks. Mammals feed their young on milk, sometimes for many months, and some continue to guard them long after they have weaned. Baby elephants stay with their mothers for years.

Time spent with parents is not wasted by youngsters. Many baby animals learn important skills from their mothers and other adults as they grow. For some, this period of learning is key to their survival in later life. Meat-eating mammals, for instance, use it as a time to hone their hunting skills, which are vital if they are to feed themselves as adults.

Animals do not stay as babies for long. Just as is often said about human children, they grow up all too quickly. While they are still babies, however, they have an incredibly magnetic appeal. All the rationalization in the world cannot overcome the emotion we feel for them.

On the Farm

*L*ambs, piglets, calves, and foals are babies
we are all familiar with. As they frolic in the fields
between our towns and cities in spring, these little
creatures are instant favorites with children. Although
they are not quite pets, they are domesticated and cared
for by people. Farmers spend their lives with them and
look after them as they grow up.

Apart from pets, farm animals are the creatures most familiar to most of us. These are the animals we learn about when we ourselves are very young. Most children know that a baby cow is called a calf and a baby pig a piglet. Even those children that have never seen one in the flesh can tell you the noises that they make.

Most of the animals we keep on farms are either mammals or birds. Baby mammals, including human babies, always seem to have large eyes. In reality, their eyes are a lot smaller than those of their parents, but they appear large because they are bigger compared to the rest of the head than those of adults. Other features, such as ears, are also exaggerated in the same way. The heads of most baby mammals are shorter and more rounded than those of their parents. This makes the process of birth slightly easier than it would otherwise be. As the babies grow up, their facial features change. Heads become longer and the shape of the skull more defined. Ears, which often look oversized on baby mammals, grow less quickly, allowing the rest of the face to catch up.

Many baby birds hatch with their eyes shut and their bodies without feathers. The chicks of chickens, however, are different. They are already quite developed by the time they hatch. Far from being stuck in the nest for weeks, they can walk from the moment they enter the world and even feed themselves, pecking instinctively at leaves and any objects on the ground that look edible.

Although baby chickens have feathers, these are not like the feathers of adults. Instead, they are soft and fluffy, a type of feather known as down. The down of these chicks serves just one purpose: keeping the baby birds warm. The more complex feathers used in flight develop later, although these are usually clipped off at the ends on domestic chickens to stop them flying away.

Many calves have pink noses when they are born, but these change color as they grow older. This little calf belongs to the Holstein breed of dairy cattle. When it starts to grow up, its nose will turn from pink to black.

Baby chickens find their own food but baby mammals rely on their mothers to provide them with milk. All baby mammals suckle and those that live on the farm are no different. The milk that we pour on our cereal in the morning is actually made by cows to feed their calves, not us. Calves on farms don't go without, however, as cows produce more milk to meet the increased demand.

Domesticated cattle have been bred to produce far more milk than their wild ancestors did. Farm cows go on producing milk long after their calves have weaned and moved on to eating grass. Occasionally calves and other farm animals may be reared by hand. This is done using large bottles of milk with specially designed teats.

▲ Baby cattle are all known as calves. As they become older, however, they acquire different names. Young females that have not calved or only calved once are known as heifers. Young males are called bullocks.

▶ Baby chickens are like little round bundles of fluff. They keep their soft downy feathers for just a few days before they begin to develop their adult plumage. Baby chickens instinctively follow their mother wherever she goes. Most hens have between 8 and 13 chicks in a single clutch.

All farm animals originally came from wild species. The ancestor of the cow was a now-extinct creature called the aurochs, which lived in the forests of Europe. Sheep are descended from another European wild animal, the mouflon. Mouflons look rather like bighorn sheep, their stocky North American cousins, but are today now much less common in the wild than those animals.

The wild ancestor of the goat was an animal known as the bezoar ibex. The descendants of this extremely nimble creature still live in mountains and other rocky habitats in Turkey and parts of the Middle East. Today's farm goats have kept their ancestors' great climbing ability. Even the youngsters, known as kids, are experts at clambering around and can balance in places few other animals would even try to go. Domesticated goats have kept another trait from the bezoar ibex, the ability to digest a wide range of plant food. Farm goats are known for trying to eat almost anything and will often nibble at the sleeves of people who come to stroke or feed them. Baby goats, of course, feed entirely on milk. Their mothers, known

Goats, like cattle, come in different breeds. Some have ears that stick up in the air but others, like this baby Nubian goat, have long, floppy ears. Baby goats are known as kids and have been so called for much longer than human children have.

Most sheep are kept for their wool, which is used to make clothing. Baby sheep, or lambs, have much shorter, finer wool than their parents. Most lambs are born singly, although occasionally ewes may give birth to twins.

as nanny goats, have two teats on their udders, as do female sheep, or ewes. Cows' udders have four teats.

Baby sheep, of course, are known as lambs. All lambs are born with long tails but these are usually docked when they are very young to prevent them getting messy as they grow older. Like many baby mammals, lambs are extremely playful and can often be seen bouncing around in the fields soon after they are born in spring.

▲ The domesticated pig is descended from the European wild boar. Wild boar piglets are stripy for camouflage but domesticated piglets vary in color. This Tamworth piglet is orangey-brown like her mother.

▲ Pigs often have quite large litters, compared with other farm animals. This is reflected by the number of teats most sows have—14 altogether. The smallest piglet in a litter is known as the runt.

◀ Cattle are grazers, eating grass and other low-growing plants. Although this calf is still young enough to be suckling milk, his mouth is broad and flat like his mother's. Browsing mammals, which pluck leaves from branches, have narrower snouts and mouths than grazers.

▲ All donkeys have big ears but those of donkey foals look huge, almost like those of a rabbit. Donkey foals, like some young cattle, have longer, denser fur than their parents. Their smaller bodies lose heat more easily and this thicker fur helps keep them warm during cold weather.

▲ Before the invention of the tractor, heavy horses were common on farms. They were used to pull plows, harrows and other farm implements. Today horses and ponies are mainly kept for riding. A baby horse is called a foal.

◄ Foals have shorter, fluffier tails than adult ponies and horses. Their bodies are shorter too, which has the effect of making their legs appear longer. Foals are usually up on their feet within an hour of being born.

► Growing quickly in the first month of life, one of the first things to change is a foal's legs, which become more muscular and stocky. Foals feed only on their mother's milk for the first few weeks and then gradually start to supplement their diet with grass.

Pads, Paws, and Claws

*N*o one would want to cuddle an adult lion
or tiger but somehow their cubs still manage to look
endearing. Young carnivores are almost like living soft
toys, with long, fluffy coats, oversized ears, and big feet.
Baby wallabies, koalas, and other marsupials have
their own appealing charm too.

Baby carnivorous mammals have more growing up to do than most. They have an awful lot to learn if they are to be successful hunters. Carnivorous mammals include all of the members of the cat, dog, bear, raccoon, and weasel families, among others. Most of them live on a diet of meat as adults. Catching prey requires a lot more skill and patience than finding plant food, such as grass.

Baby carnivorous mammals learn to hunt through play. They instinctively stalk or chase almost anything that moves. Lion cubs often practice their skills by sneaking up and pouncing on their mothers' tails. Other popular targets include buzzing insects and leaves blowing in the wind.

Carnivorous mammals spend much longer with their mothers than most animals do. When they are very young, she suckles them, and later she brings them meat. By watching her and mimicking her behavior, they slowly learn all they need to catch prey on their own. Only once they are completely independent does she drive them away, sometimes as much as two years after they were born.

Most carnivorous mammals, including many big cat species such as leopards and lynx are mainly solitary hunters but not all of them live like this. Lions, for instance, live and hunt in groups known as prides. These are ruled over by a dominant male, or occasionally two or three males which are usually brothers. Adult males come and go from a pride—they stay only as long as they are able to, eventually being driven off and replaced by younger, more vigorous males. Most females, on the other hand, stay with the pride for life. They arrive as newborn cubs and continue to stay once they are adults. Male lion cubs, by contrast, are forced to leave the pride by their father as they approach adulthood. They spend several years alone or with brothers until they are big enough to challenge a dominant male and fight to rule a pride of their own.

◀ The bobcat or bay lynx comes from North America and is one of the smaller cat species. Its offspring are known as kittens. The young are taught by their mother to hunt and will be weaned at around two months of age. Before their first winter they are able to hunt by themselves and will leave in search of their own territory.

▶ This little wolf cub has only recently left the den, but already he looks fearless. Young wolf cubs are extremely well looked after, both by their mother and by the other members of the pack.

▼ Female lions give birth to litters of between one to six cubs. Pride females suckle one another's cubs, with no bias toward their own and weaning is completed by the time the young are six months old.

Wolves, like lions, also live and hunt in groups. Wolves are members of the dog family and are the species from which our own pet dogs are descended. Wolf packs are dominated by a single breeding pair. (In lion prides all of the adult females mate with the male and have cubs). The other adult wolves in the pack are usually grown-up cubs born to this pair. These grown-up cubs help both with hunting and bringing up their younger brothers and sisters.

Wolf cubs, like puppies, are born blind and helpless. Their eyes only open once they are about two weeks old. Before they are born, their mother finds a secluded den. Here she gives birth and suckles them, relying on her mate and other pack members to bring her food. Once they are around a month old, the cubs start eating meat but they continue to suckle as well for a few more weeks.

Tiger cubs may look cuddly but they are actually quite strong. Even when they are small like this, they have long, pointed teeth and fearsome claws. Tigers, like most cats, keep their claws sharp by retracting them into their paws when at rest or walking. They only unsheathe their claws when necessary, pulling them forward with specialized muscles.

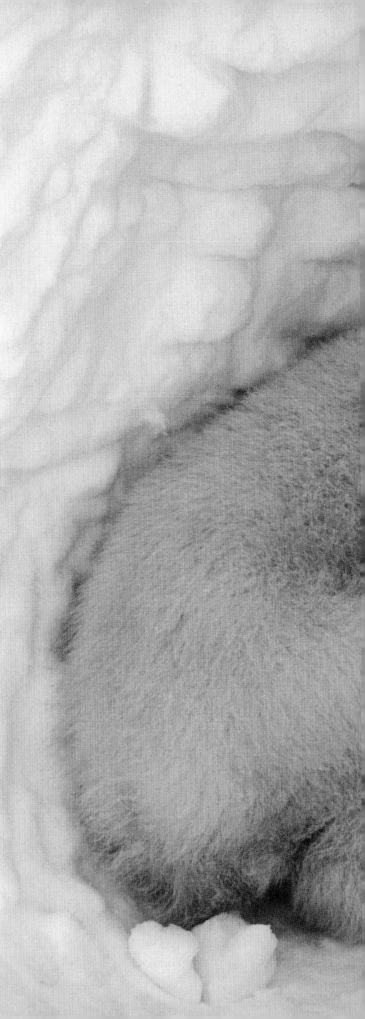

They leave the den at about six weeks of age and follow their mother, who introduces them to the rest of the pack. Older wolf cubs help raise their siblings by guarding them when their mother and the rest of the pack is out hunting. They are also very patient playmates, joining in rough and tumble games with the young cubs.

Baby bears are also known as cubs and they too are born in dens. Unlike wolves, however, their mothers go without food until the cubs are big enough to face the outside world. Bears are solitary animals and a female's mate plays no part in feeding her or helping bring up their young.

Bear cubs, like wolves, are born blind and helpless. For the first few days they can only crawl around the den slowly, but as they grow bigger, their eyes open and they push themselves up on their paws and start walking. They stay in the den with their mother for a few weeks before venturing outside. Once she has fed herself, they get their first taste of solid food.

▲ Polar bears give birth to one, two, or three cubs beneath the snow in the depths of winter. By the time spring arrives, the cubs are big enough to follow their mother across the icy wastes of the Arctic, where she continues to provide for them and keep them warm.

▶ The cubs are born in a snow den, safe from the attentions of predators. Their pure white coats both keep them warm and help them to blend in with their surroundings. Soon they leave the security of the den to explore the outside world.

Bears are classified as carnivores but only the polar bear lives exclusively on meat. Other bears supplement their diet with roots, berries and other plant matter. One bear-like creature, the giant panda, lives entirely on plant matter. Some scientists classify this creature as a bear, while others think that it belongs in the raccoon family. Either way, the giant panda has long claws and formidable teeth, but it only uses these for gathering and munching bamboo. Baby giant pandas suckle milk until they are about eight or nine months old and only gradually move on to eating bamboo, which is tough, low in nutrients and difficult to digest.

Another vegetarian sometimes called a bear is the koala. This Australian mammal, which eats the leaves of eucalyptus trees, is not actually a bear at all but a marsupial, a member of the same group as wombats, wallabies, and kangaroos. Like most marsupials, the koala has a pouch in which it carries its young. Marsupial babies are born when they are very tiny and barely have limbs, let alone hair. Once they have found their way into the pouch, they latch on to a nipple and do not let go for several weeks.

▲ *Baby giant pandas have to be among the most endearing of all animal babies, looking just like big, living soft toys. Their seemingly bold colors actually provide them with good camouflage amongst the snow and rocks of the hills and mountains where they come from in China. Sadly, they are now quite rare in the wild.*

◀ *Baby koalas remain hidden in their mother's pouch for about six months. During this time they grow ears, eyes, and fur. The joey then begins to explore outside of the pouch. The infant will remain with its mother for another six months or so, riding on her back, and feeding on both milk and eucalyptus leaves until weaned at about 12 months of age.*

▶ *The North American black bear also comes in shades of brown, as this youngster shows. Black bear cubs are great climbers and instantly head up into the trees at the first sign of danger.*

▲ Fox cubs waste no time in learning to hunt. Almost as soon as they can walk, they start exploring the world around them and take a great interest in anything that moves. Play-hunting beetles and other insects is good practice. One day this cub will have to hunt on its own to survive.

▲ All raccoons are naturally inquisitive, but the youngsters are especially so. Learning to climb is important for baby raccoons. As adults they will find much of their food off the ground.

▶ Young cheetah cubs learn how to hunt from their mother. When they grow up, they will be the fastest land animals on Earth, capable of sprinting at speeds of up to 63mph (100km/h).

▲ Baby kangaroos are known as joeys. This female joey is taking her first steps. Joeys spend the first 10 or 11 months of life in their mother's pouch. Even after they have left the pouch they continue to suckle for several months.

◀ This fluffy-looking baby is better protected than it might at first appear. It is a young North American porcupine and already has short, sharp spines beneath its longer hairs.

▶ Meerkats are small carnivores belonging to the mongoose family. Unlike most mongooses they are sociable animals, living in groups of up to 30 individuals. Baby meerkats are guarded by 'babysitters' while the rest of the group is out foraging for food. When they are about four weeks old they begin joining the foraging parties themselves.

Born to Run

*S*ome babies are quicker to get up on their feet than others. Baby antelopes and other plant eaters must be able to run as soon as possible if they are to stay safe from predators. They also need to be fast enough to keep up with their mother as she wanders in a continual search for new grass and other leafy food.

Plant-eating mammals rarely have to look far for food. Most of them live surrounded by everything they need—grazers have food right at their feet almost wherever they go. Life is not all easy for these creatures, however, as they themselves are potential food for meat-eating animals. To survive, they have to be quick on their feet and constantly alert.

Most plant-eating mammals that live in the open can run within hours of being born. Although they are too young to know what sights, sounds, and smells signal danger, these babies instinctively follow what their mother does. If she starts running, they run along with her. Baby deer and antelopes in particular can be surprisingly fast.

For many plant eaters, running is their only protection, but for some there are other options if predators approach. Large animals, such as elephants and rhinos, might stop in their tracks, turn, and charge. Their sheer size can be enough to frighten most meat-eating animals away. Baby rhinos instinctively stick close to their mother and she defends her young fiercely from any animals she sees as posing a threat. Baby elephants are even better protected. Their mothers live as part of larger groups and every member of the group takes care to guard its youngest members. If elephants are threatened by lions or other animals, they form a defensive ring with the babies at the center. Faced by a bellowing wall of tusks and trunks, all but the bravest and hungriest predators tend to back down.

Elephants are not the only animals to defend their young in this way. In the frozen wastes of the Arctic, herds of musk-oxen protect their calves in exactly the same manner, forming a circle around their babies. Musk-oxen have one main predator, the Arctic wolf, a subspecies of the gray wolf which lives farther south. These animals are powerful predators but they tend to hunt alone or in very small packs. With their large horns, musk-oxen are well defended and by sticking together they are usually able to drive wolves away.

◀ *Baby deer are known as fawns or calves. Most deer give birth to just a single youngster each year, although occasionally twins are born. Like most hoofed mammals, baby deer are quickly up on their feet.*

Even the most advanced babies are a little unsteady when they are born. While their mothers might give them encouragement, they cannot actually help them to stand up—they have to do that all on their own. For baby deer, cattle, and antelopes standing up is important for more than one reason. While they must quickly learn to master their legs to keep themselves safe from predators, they also have to stand up in order to feed. All of these animals suckle their young while they themselves are up on their feet. If a youngster is to get its first meal of milk, it also has to stand up to reach a teat.

▲ *Africa is home to many different species of antelope. This picture shows a mother impala with her calf. Unlike some female antelopes, impala females lack horns.*

▶ *One of the first things most baby antelopes do when they get to their feet is try to suckle. This newborn springbok has the right idea but has not found the right spot yet. All baby mammals are damp when they are born and most, like this one, still have part of the umbilical cord attached.*

A few plant-eating mammals avoid the problem of predators by having their young underground. Rabbits, for instance, give birth to their babies in burrows, out of sight of predators and largely safe from danger. Baby rabbits are born blind, naked, and helpless and suckle in the darkness for three or four weeks before they are big and strong enough to face the outside world. Hares, which do not dig burrows but give birth on the surface, have babies that are much more developed. Baby hares, known as leverets, are born fully furred and with their eyes open. Their mother gives birth to them under a bush or in another similarly secluded spot and often leaves them soon after they have been born to feed herself. If they sense danger, the leverets lie low and freeze, only daring to move again once they feel it has passed. If they are discovered, they can run, although not as quickly as the adults can.

Litters of up to seven baby rabbits are born underground in burrows. They are naked, blind, and helpless at birth, but they grow rapidly, and are usually weaned in about four weeks.

Roe deer are common in Britain and Europe. Unlike many deer, they live alone or in pairs rather than in herds. This roe deer fawn is lying still in the hope that it will not be seen, relying on its coat for camouflage.

Baby hoofed mammals often have legs that look too long for their bodies, giving them a gangly appearance. This is not an accident of nature but has evolved for the reason of self-preservation. Having longer legs means that these babies can run faster, helping them to avoid predators and keep up with their mothers if they find themselves being chased. Many newborn antelopes have legs more than two-thirds the length of those of fully grown adults.

Not all baby hoofed mammals run at the first sign of danger. Some, particularly those that live in wooded areas, hide. Often these babies are patterned to help them blend in with their surroundings and avoid being seen. Baby deer often have coats that are covered in spots, even though those of their parents are plain.

▲ Bison calves have much lighter-colored fur than their parents, but it is thick and woolly to help keep their bodies warm. Bison once roamed right across central North America but today they are confined mainly to National Parks and other nature reserves.

▶ Although it looks rather like a cow, the wildebeest is a type of antelope. Wildebeest form huge herds which make great migrations every year across the African savannah in search of new grazing. The newborn calves are soon on their feet and able to follow their mothers on the arduous journey across the plains.

▲ Like many hoofed mammals, giraffes give birth standing up, so baby giraffes enter the world with a thud, falling almost 7ft (2m) to the savannah floor. Once they are up on their feet, these tall babies soon learn to suckle, bending their long necks to get at their mothers' teats.

▶ Giraffes have evolved to feed on the leaves of the few trees that grow on the African savannah, a source of food out of reach of most other animals. They are famous for being the world's tallest land animals. Even so, a giraffe only has seven bones in its neck, the same number as a human.

◀ This baby white rhino looks rather grumpy, but he will have that expression for the rest of his life. White rhinos are not white at all— the name comes from the Afrikaans word 'wijd,' meaning wide, which refers to the shape of the animal's mouth.

▲ Zebras are wild members of the horse family. Zebra foals are born with their characteristic stripy coats. These help to break up the outlines of individual animals in a moving herd, making it harder for predators to target them.

▶ *Elephant calves are suckled by their mothers but are cared for and protected by all of the members of the herd. Elephant herds are made up of adult females, juvenile animals, and calves. Herds are led by the oldest female, known as the matriarch. Bull elephants live largely solitary lives and only join up with herds briefly to breed. They play no part in looking after the young.*

Monkey Magic

Apes and monkeys are primates just like
us and their babies often look almost human, with an
intelligence in their eyes that we recognize. When they
are very young, they are completely dependent on
their mothers but as they grow older, they become
more adventurous and mischievous, just
like our own children do.

*B*aby primates have a quality we can relate to. After all, human beings are primates too. Primates comprise a group of related mammals, classified as a family by zoologists. They include some of the most intelligent and inquisitive animals on Earth. Monkeys are primates, as are apes and lemurs.

Primates are born with a few instinctive behaviors but they are completely dependent on their mothers for food, transport and protection. Like all mammals, they start out life feeding on milk, then gradually move on to a diet of solids. Primates have an advantage over many other animals in that they have a greater capacity to learn. Babies discover what is good to eat and what should be left alone by watching their mothers. They also learn from them where to find it. Some primate species concentrate on just a few sources of food but many have extremely varied diets. Orang utans, for example, eat more than 200 types of fruit. By the age of ten, an orang utan can recognize every one of these and find them, despite the fact that they are scattered through the forest. This is an incredible feat of learning, especially considering the fact that different trees in the tropical rainforests where orang utans live fruit at different times of the year. These apes learn not only what to eat and where it grows but when to go to those places and gather it.

Baby primates go wherever their mothers take them. From the moment they are born, they cling tightly to her fur. Some ride on their mothers' backs and others hang underneath. Only when they have reached a certain size do they begin exploring the world around them and even then their mothers are never far away. As soon as it is time to move on, the mother sweeps her baby up in her arms and he or she holds on, ready to be carried to wherever she is heading next.

◀ *A baby squirrel monkey sleeps on her mother's back. Squirrel monkeys come from South America and are carried around until they are about three months old. Births occur at the time of year when rainfall is at its heaviest.*

In a few primate species, it is the fathers who carry the young around most of the time. Some marmosets and tamarins, very small monkeys from South America, do this. When they are very young, the babies need regular feeds of milk and so are carried by their mothers, but as soon as they are big enough, they are passed to their father.

Most primates stay as babies and youngsters for quite a long time. Some take several years to grow up completely. Apes, the group to which humans belong, take the longest of all. Gorillas do not reach their full size until they are about 10 or 11 years old. Chimpanzees take even longer, with males finally becoming adults when they are about 15. These long, extended childhoods give primates the time they need not just to grow but to acquire the knowledge and develop the skills they must possess for adult life. For many, these include social skills as well as those necessary for finding food. Gorillas, chimps and most monkeys are group-living animals. While living in groups has its benefits in terms of protection from predators, it also has challenges. As part of the process of growing up, babies must learn their place in the social hierarchy and get to know how to deal with other individuals.

Of course, not all primates live in big groups. Orang utans have largely solitary lives as adults, except for mothers with their young. Gibbons have another social structure, living in families almost like our own. The mother and father stick together for years, sometimes for life, and raise their young until they too are on the verge of becoming adults. The adolescents then 'leave home,' being driven out of the family territory. In time, with luck, each youngster finds a partner. These couples then start families and establish new territories of their own.

▶ *This ring-tailed lemur is carrying twins. Lemurs come from Madagascar, a large island off the east coast of Africa, and are found nowhere else in the world. They are among the most primitive living primates.*

Gibbons are among the most athletic of all primates, swinging hand over hand through the high branches of the South-East Asian rainforests where they live. As with all primates, their first forays into the branches are closely watched, with their mother near enough to offer a helping hand if they find themselves in difficulty. Learning to climb is a process that most young primates undergo, even those that are destined to spend the majority of their adult life on the ground. There is an instinctive joy in scrambling through the branches that our own species has retained, at least as children. Where trees are in short supply, we tend to provide our own offspring with climbing frames.

Gibbon babies such as this little creature, go from small, helpless-looking bundles of fur clinging on to their mothers to arboreal acrobats in the space of two years.

Orang utans live on the islands of Sumatra and Borneo. They are Asia's largest wild apes and spend almost all of their lives in the trees. The name orang utan is Malay and translates literally as 'man of the forest'. Baby orang utans live with their mothers until they are around 8 years old.

A tiny baby vervet monkey plays in the grass. When they are born, vervet monkeys have pink faces and ears, but these turn black as they grow older. Vervet monkeys live in groups known as troops, which may have up to 50 members.

Baby chimpanzees look almost human. These African apes are actually our closest living relatives, sharing more than 98 percent of our DNA. Like us, they have complex social relationships and are omnivores, eating both plant matter and meat.

A sleepy newborn gorilla baby rests on his mother's chest. Gorillas are the largest living primates of all: adult males can weigh up to 605lb (275kg). Despite their somewhat intimidating appearance, gorillas are largely peaceful apes and entirely vegetarian.

▲ *The little creature above is a baby baboon. Baboons, like vervets, are African monkeys. Baboons, however, are larger and spend more of their time on the ground.*

◀ *A young baboon rides on her mother's back. This youngster is a few weeks older than the baby above. Baboons live and travel in large troops led by several dominant males. These males have large canine teeth and work together to protect the troop from predators such as leopards. They also keep order within the troop, breaking up quarrels between females and other subordinate members.*

Water Babies

Some young animals are born to swim.
Seal pups spend their first days on land with their
mother but quickly grow big enough to enter the sea.
Other water babies, such as turtles, start life on their
own. For them, the challenges of the ocean must be
overcome alone, without the help of a parent to
protect and guide them.

*A*ll sorts of animals live in the water. Some, such as fish, are found nowhere else, but others have many more relatives on land and are descended from land-living ancestors. Seals, dolphins, and whales are aquatic mammals. Like all mammals, they breathe air and so must return to the surface every so often to fill their lungs. Aquatic reptiles also rely on air for their oxygen. Unlike fish, which have gills, they cannot extract it from the water around them.

Many aquatic mammals and reptiles have their babies on land. Seals and sea lions haul out every spring to pup. Most choose isolated beaches or ice floes where they are safe from land-living predators. Some haul out in small numbers but many form huge, noisy colonies with hundreds of mothers and young. Adult males, known as bulls, are found in these colonies too, on the lookout for females with which to breed.

Seal and sea lion pups are fed rich milk and grow up very quickly. Most are able to swim and enter the sea within a few weeks of birth. Some seals in cold climates have pups with white furry coats. These camouflage the babies against the snow and also help to keep them warm. Most seal pups quickly build up a layer of fat, or blubber, beneath their skin. This gives them much greater protection from the cold and they shed their baby fur before starting life in the sea.

Most aquatic creatures, of course, lay their eggs or have young in the water itself. With a few very unusual exceptions, this is true of all fish. Most fish shed their eggs into the water and then leave them but some take great care of their eggs and their young. Many cichlids, for example, pick their fertilized eggs up in their mouths and move them to the gill cavities near the back, where they can incubate protected from predators. Seahorses, perhaps the strangest-looking fish of all, have an even more unusual system. The male seahorse has a pouch on his belly in which the eggs are held until they hatch. Young seahorses, sometimes known as ponies, stay near their father until they are quite large.

A bottlenose dolphin swims with her baby. Dolphins give birth in the water and the mother helps her baby to the surface to take its first breath. Dolphins usually have just a single youngster at a time. Like all mammals, they feed their offspring on milk.

▲ This baby tree frog has only recently lost the stub of its tadpole tail and left the water. Tree frogs are adept climbers, as their name suggests. Their toes have sticky pads which enable them to cling on to plant stems and leaves.

▶ Even alligators look cute when they are small. Female alligators actually make surprisingly good parents, guarding their nests from would-be egg thieves and gently carrying their offspring down to the water in their mouths after they hatch.

Turtles and crocodiles leave the water to have their babies, but, rather than giving birth to live young, they lay eggs. Mating between these aquatic reptiles occurs in the water and only the females emerge when the time for nesting arrives. Sea turtles, like seals and sea lions, prefer isolated beaches. They usually come out of the sea at night, often in large numbers, and dig pits in the sand into which they lay their eggs. Once they have finished laying, they use their flippers to cover the clutch up with sand and then make their way back to the sea. The eggs are left to incubate on their own. They hatch a few weeks later and the babies dig their way out of the sand and scramble down the beach toward the waves.

A mother and baby hippo raise their eyes above the surface to have a look around. Hippos come out on to land at night to graze but spend the hot daylight hours in the water. They are found throughout most of Africa south of the Sahara.

The capybara is the world's largest rodent, with adult males growing to be as big as sheep. Capybaras come from South America and spend much of their time in the water, finding safety there from predators such as jaguars.

This harbor seal mother and pup are lying in the surf zone on a beach in California. Harbor seals are among the most widespread of all seal species. They also live around the shores of Britain and Europe, where they are known as common seals.

▲ This killer whale calf is just a few days old. Killer whales are intelligent, social animals that live in groups known as pods. A killer whale pod may contain more than 20 individual animals, which work together as a unit to locate and hunt prey.

◀ A humpback whale calf travels with his mother. Whales have the largest babies on Earth. The biggest of all is the calf of the blue whale, measuring 23ft (7m) long and weighing up to 3 tons at birth.

▲ This endearing creature is a young beluga or white whale. Belugas are unusual among whales in being able to move their lips. They are among the most vocal of all marine mammals, a fact that has earned them another name—sea canaries.

Feathered Friends

Few parents work harder than birds.
*Their youngsters seem to be constantly hungry, their
big mouths wide open to gulp the next meal. Not all
baby birds rely on their parents to feed them, however.
Ducklings and some other chicks can find food for
themselves straight away and leave the
nest while still very young.*

Baby birds enter the world as eggs. Before they take their first breath, they grow and develop inside a protective shell, incubated by the warmth of their mother's body. In some species the father helps out with incubation too, covering the eggs while his mate goes in search of a meal.

Eggs need to be kept warm for the chicks inside them to develop. They are only left uncovered for short periods of time, as parents swap over incubation duties or if one of them senses danger. Some birds sit tight on their eggs until the last minute but others leave the nest to dive-bomb potential predators or make themselves look like targets to lure them away. The eggs themselves are often well camouflaged, particularly those of bird species that nest on the ground. This means that even if the parents are temporarily driven off by a predator, the eggs may still go undetected.

Most birds go to some lengths to protect their eggs. Many nest in secluded spots or high up in branches where most predators cannot reach. Seabirds tend to nest on cliff ledges or on isolated islands. Those that are forced to lay their eggs on the ground because of the habitat in which they live are usually very well camouflaged, to avoid drawing attention to themselves and the nest.

Most birds incubate their eggs for just a few weeks, although a few, such as some penguins and albatrosses, do so for more than two months. While it is being incubated, the growing chick inside each egg uses the yolk as its source of food. Eventually, with the yolk almost used up, the chick is ready to hatch.

A chick hatches by tapping away at the inside of its egg with its beak. Eventually the shell cracks and the baby bird is able to force its way out. Some chicks hatch with their eyes shut and their bodies naked, without feathers. Others are much more developed, with their eyes open and their bodies covered with down.

◀ *Baby swans are known as cygnets. Like most waterfowl, they are able to swim straight away. When they get tired, small cygnets clamber up on to their mother's back for a free ride and a rest.*

▲ Most chicks spend their first weeks in a nest and rely on their parents to bring them food. This mother has made it difficult for predators to reach her chicks by building her nest out on the end of a narrow twig.

▶ Many young birds continue to be fed even after they have left the nest. This fledgling could almost be mistaken for an adult but is given away by the fleshy corners of its mouth, which emphasize its gape when it opens its mouth for food.

The least developed chicks at hatching tend to be those incubated in nests off the ground. These babies rely on their parents entirely for weeks to come. Mother and father make almost continuous round trips to fill their hungry beaks with food. Slowly the chicks grow and develop downy feathers. Next their eyes open and finally adult feathers begin to replace their down. As they grow, the chicks become more active and practice flapping their wings near the edge of the nest. Weeks after hatching, they are able to take their first flight. Even then, however, they continue to rely on their parents to bring them food. With the last vestiges of fluffy down still visible, they perch in the branches and beg. Complete independence only comes when they have learned to find food on their own.

Most ground-nesting birds have chicks that are much quicker to leave the nest. Young pheasants and plovers, for instance, can not only see but can walk almost from the

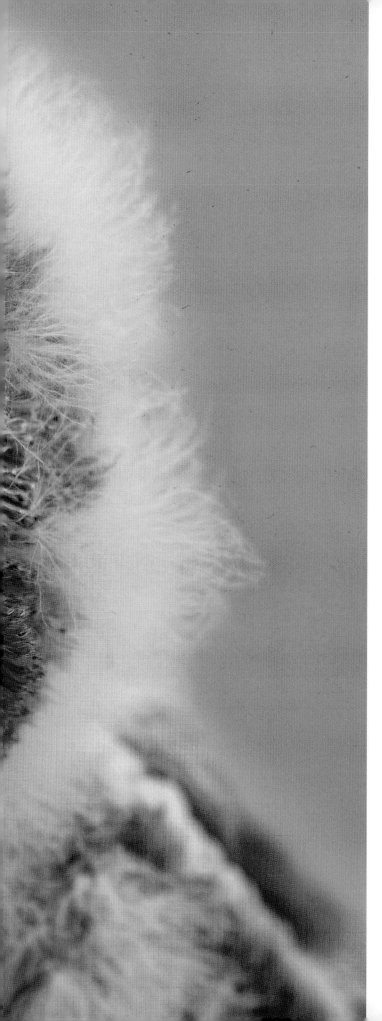

moment they hatch. These babies instinctively start to feed themselves, pecking at leaves and anything small resembling food that moves on the ground.

Although these babies do not need their parents to feed them, they do rely on them for protection. They follow the adults wherever they go. In some species, both parents guard the young from danger. In other species, the father leaves once the eggs have hatched and the mother looks after the chicks on her own.

Waterfowl have chicks that are equally precocious. Ducklings, goslings, and cygnets can not only walk but swim within hours of hatching. Like baby pheasants and plovers, they are covered with fluffy down which serves to keep them warm. As they grow larger, this down gives way to adult feathers, until eventually they are fully fledged.

▲ *This young oriole has almost completely lost the downy feathers it had as a chick—just a few tufts remain. Woodland birds, orioles feed on fruit and insects which they find high up in the trees.*

◀ *Owls are unable to move their eyes but they compensate for this in an extraordinary manner—they can twist their necks until they can see in every direction! This scruffy-looking youngster is a barn owl.*

Baby waterfowl are unable to fly for weeks but this is no handicap when it comes to finding food. Some peck at water plants while others, including most goslings, graze out on land. If danger threatens, they and the mother goose head for the water, where few predators can follow.

Most seabird chicks stay on land until they have gained their adult plumage. While the majority hatch with their eyes open and their bodies covered with down, they rely on their parents to bring them back meals from the sea. Some seabird parents, such as puffins, carry fish in their beaks. Others, such as penguins, swallow their catch and then regurgitate it for their young when they get back to shore.

▲ *A mother goose takes her goslings out on the water. Goslings usually stay close to their parents, who guard them fiercely from any animal that comes too close. Geese are so protective of their young that they will sometimes even attack people.*

▶ *This little gosling is the young of a Canada goose. Canada geese, as their name suggests, are native to North America. In the 17th century the species was introduced to South-East England and has since spread to become one of the most common water birds in Britain, around lakes and parks.*

A guillemot chick waits for his mother to return with a meal of fish. Guillemots nest in large colonies on cliffs around the North Atlantic Ocean in spring, sharing the ledges with razorbills, kittiwakes, and other seabirds.

Emperor penguins raise their chicks on the Antarctic ice. The male incubates the single egg on his feet, covered with his brood pouch, through the depths of winter, only returning to the sea to feed when relieved in spring by his mate.

Flamingoes are filter feeders, straining tiny organisms from the water with their bizarre-looking beaks. Mother flamingoes feed their young with a red, milk-like substance which they secrete from their upper digestive tract.

Perfect Pets

Puppies, kittens, guinea pigs, hamsters—these little creatures share our lives and our homes. The baby animals we know best are the ones that we live with and make our pets. We give them warmth, shelter, food, and affection. They repay us by becoming dependable friends or even loyal members of our families.

There are few things in the world cuter than a puppy or kitten. People love baby animals so much that they bring them into their homes and care for them as pets.

Baby pets are unusual in being brought up by humans rather than by their own kind. They are often taken into the family when they are only just weaned. As long as baby pets are given enough love and are well looked after, they quickly become attached to their owners. They learn to recognize the people they live with and often follow them around.

Some pets become more independent than others as they grow older—cats, for instance, are quite happy to spend time on their own. Pet cats are descended from the African wild cat, which is a largely solitary creature. Dogs, on the other hand, crave company and get upset if they are left alone for too long. Their ancestors, wolves, are pack animals. Dogs see the humans they live with as part of their pack and they are happiest when the pack is together.

Most of the animals people keep as pets are mammals. They are warm, furry creatures that enjoy being stroked. Some, such as guinea pigs and rabbits, tend to be kept in their own little cage or enclosure, and are only taken out occasionally for exercise in the garden or to be handled. Others, such as cats and dogs, usually have the run of the house.

Just as baby wild animals learn to hunt or find food for themselves by watching their mothers, so baby pets can be trained to behave in certain ways or learn tricks. Puppies are particularly good learners. If they are rewarded with treats or a pat, they can be taught how to do all sorts of things. Most pet dogs are taught to sit and to come when called, but some learn to obey many other commands. Sheepdogs, for instance, can be taught to understand different combinations of calls and whistling sounds, which shepherds use to direct them when rounding up sheep. These dogs are both pets and working partners. Without them, shepherds would find their jobs much more difficult.

Golden retriever puppies have a look that just asks to be loved. These youngsters will grow up into gentle, good-natured dogs. Golden retrievers are good with children and make wonderful family pets.

Over the years, dogs have been bred into a huge variety of different shapes and forms. Today, there are almost 200 recognized breeds of dog. Most dogs were originally bred to do particular jobs. Hounds, for instance, were used for hunting. Terriers were also used for catching animals, although the creatures they caught were usually smaller than those chased by hounds. Others were bred for rounding up and protecting livestock. Only a few breeds, the toy dogs, were actually bred to be pets. Toy dogs include many of the smallest breeds, such as the Pekingese, Chihuahua and King Charles spaniel.

Today, of course, most dogs are kept as pets. Among the most popular are those that were originally bred as gundogs, for flushing out and fetching game birds. These include the majority of spaniels and retrievers, such as Labradors. They still enjoy fetching objects and bringing them back to their owners but nowadays most chase and pick up frisbees, rubber balls, or sticks.

▲ *This West Highland terrier puppy is a tiny bundle of fun. Even when he is fully grown, he will be less than 1ft (30cm) tall. As a baby he is little bigger than a grown-up guinea pig. West Highland terriers were originally bred in Scotland, as their name suggests.*

A pair of Jack Russell terrier puppies snooze curled up together. Jack Russells are named for the man who created the breed in the early 1800s. A parson from Devonshire in South-West England, he bred them to be small enough to flush foxes from their burrows, known as earths.

Guinea pigs originally came from South America and are descended from wild cavies. Today there are dozens of different domesticated breeds of various colors, and many with long fur.

Baby rabbits are born blind and hairless. However, they soon grow a coat of fur, open their eyes, and start exploring the world around them. Baby rabbits are known as kits. At first their ears are quite small, but they become longer as the babies grow up.

▲ These kittens have curled up together in their bed. After an energetic time exploring and playing, kittens need plenty of rest and will sleep for a total of 12 to 15 hours per day.

◀ Kittens sometimes seem to have courage beyond their age and their diminutive size does not impede their inquisitive nature. They enjoy playing with toys and will chase butterflies and leaves as they practice their hunting skills.

▶ As kittens grow, they lose their chunky baby shape. One thing they never lose, however, is their fearless nature, which seems to be written on this kitten's face.

▲ This little puppy belongs to a breed of toy dog known as the Bichon Frisé. As she gets older her fur will grow until it is long enough to reach the ground. There are over 20 recognized breeds of toy dog altogether.

▶ Husky puppies have piercing blue eyes like their parents. Huskies are perhaps the hardiest dogs of all. They were originally bred in Siberia and are often used in teams to pull sledges in Arctic conditions.

*I*ndex

Picture Credits *(l=left, r=right, a=above, b=below, c=center)*

© Shutterstock.com: asian 88-89; Till von Au 17*(br)*; Marilyn Barbone 80-81*(l)*; Baloncici 75*(c)*; Jessica Bethke 36*(r)*; Joy Brown 94; Karel Brož 42-43*(l)*; Tony Campbell 31; Christian Charisius 58; Stephanie Coffman 19; Tom Curtis 84*(a)*; Richard F. Cox 63*(r)*; Waldemar Dabrowski 86, 90*(a)*; Pedro Diaz 65*(c)*; Ecliptic Blue 1, 61*(a)*; Holger Ehlers 4*(c)*; Tim Elliot 82; Richard Fitzer 47; Steffen Foerster Photography 62-63*(l)*; Chris Fourie 44-45*(r)*; Daniel Gale 18*(b)*; Eric Gevaert 53*(l)*, 53*(r)*, 54-55, 56-57; Kaspars Grinvalds 30*(b)*; Gertjan Hooijer 5*(l)*; Jenny Horne 76-77; Dee Hunter 24*(l)*; Image Plan 64; Laila Kazakevica 60; Yan Ke 73*(b)*; Gunta Klavina 75*(r)*; Klaus Rainer Krieger 68*(l)*; Foong Kok Leong 15; Craig Mills 37*(l)*; David Nagy 84*(b)*; Petspicture 92*(b)*; Photobar 40; Plastique 95; Dusan Po 5; Vladimir Popovic 90*(b)*; Brent Reeves 71; Mostakov Roman 74; Ronen 78-79*(r)*; Jean Schweitzer 92*(a)*, front endpaper; Kristian Sekulic 21*(l)*, 65*(r)*; Chin Kit Sen 20; Wong Tsu Shi 78*(l)*; Steve Snowden 12-13*(r)*; SouWest Photography 7, 50-51; Johan Swanepoel 4*(r)*, 36; Jeff Thrower 87*(c)*; Chris Turner 4*(l)*; Julie Turner 91*(a)*; Beth Van Trees 80; Gerrit de Vries 52; Webtrias 22-23; Wolfgang Zintl 75*(r)*.

© iStockphoto.com: iStock 40-41*(r)*; Eduardo Alarcon 12*(l)*; Atwag 9*(r)*; Kitch Bain 30*(a)*; Simone van den Berg 87*(l)*, 93; Ramsey Blacklock 35*(a)*; Flavia Bottazzini 8, 70*(b)*; Sascha Burkurd 10-11; Andrew Cribb 37*(c)*; Jan Daly 73*(a)*; Betsy Dupuis 87*(r)*; Holger Ehlers 32*(b)*; Susan Evans 32-33*(r)*; Veigo Evard 14; Steffen Foerster 21*(r)*; Jill Fromer 16; Anthony Gaudio 9*(l)*; Jim Jurica 53*(c)*; Klaas Lingbeek van Kranen 21*(c)*; Scott Leman 82; Ralph Loesche 91*(b)*; Thierry Maffeis*(l)*; Neal McClimon 35*(b)*; Sue McDonald 5*(c)*; Mydarkroom 32*(a)*; Frank Parker 46; Joanna Pecha 38-39; John Pitcher 34; Hansjoerg Richter 70*(a)*; RT Images 18*(a)*; Victor Soares 49; Step2626 back endpaper; Stephen Walls 9*(c)*; Craig Walsh 17*(ar)*.

© Corbis: W. Perry Conway 26-27; Daniel J. Cox 24-25*(r)*; Tim Davis 2-3, 85; DLILLC 59; Dan Guravich 28*(l)*; Paul Hanna 66-67; Martin Harvey 48; Amos Nachoum 72-73*(l)*; Stan Osolinski 68-69*(l)*; Jenny E. Ross 28-29*(r)*; Andy Rouse 65*(l)*; Phil Schermeister 44*(l)*; Steve & Ann Toon 43*(r)*; Robert Vos 61*(b)*.

The author and publishers have made every reasonable effort to credit all copyright holders. Any errors or omissions that may have occurred are inadvertent and anyone who for any reason has not been credited is invited to write to the publishers so that a full acknowledgement may be made in subsequent editions of this work.

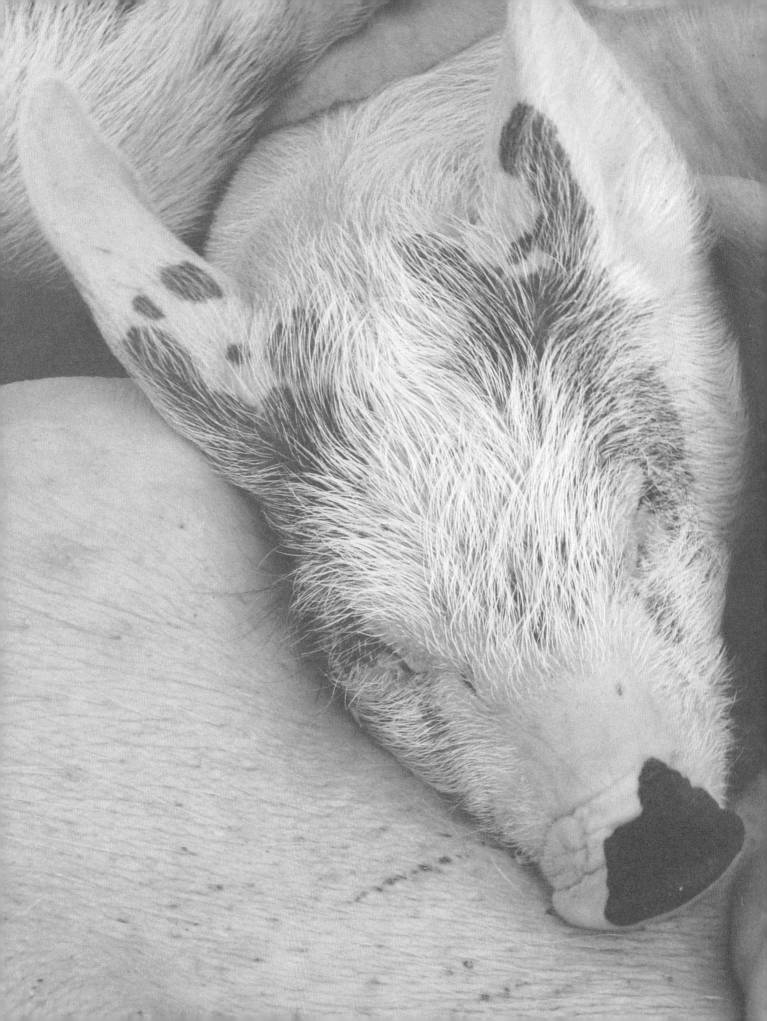